Shohsanam Ermanbetova
Ahmadjon Muhtorjonov

Habib Sadulla

Shohsanam Ermanbetova
Ahmadjon Muhtorjonov

Habib Sadulla

The book about the poet's life

JustFiction Edition

Cover image: www.ingimage.com

Publisher:
JustFiction! Edition
is a trademark of
Dodo Books Indian Ocean Ltd. and OmniScriptum S.R.L publishing group

120 High Road, East Finchley, London, N2 9ED, United Kingdom
Str. Armeneasca 28/1, office 1, Chisinau MD-2012, Republic of Moldova, Europe
Printed at: see last page
ISBN: 978-620-6-74306-4

Habib Sadulla (1942.5.4, Namangan) was editor of "Mushtum" magazine (1966-67), literary employee of the school students' newspaper (1967-68), department head, deputy editor of "Namangan Haqiqiti" newspaper (1968-73), Chairman of the Writers' Union of Namangan Region (1973-90), Head of the Regional Department of Cultural Affairs (1990-98). The first collection of poems is "Breeze from the Ocean" (in collaboration with Usman Temur, 1969). After that, Habib Sadulla's "Conversation with Spring" (1975), "Dialogue" (1979), "Again with you" (1982), "Respect" (1984), "Our Child of Gardens" (1988), "Tazarru", "From My Street" (1992), "Kosonsoy Caravans" (1993), "Uchkurgon's Three Threshing" (1996), "Ramazan Prayer" (1997), "Qadri nur" (1998) were published poetry books. The poet's epics "Year of my birth", "My mother" and "Living victims" are autobiographical. In addition, Habib Sadulla also wrote epics such as "Atlas of sky", "The Voice of the Earth", "The Seventh Continent", "Trust", "The Tale of Chust Village", "The Fate of the Writer", . Habib Sadulla's dramas "Yusuf and Zulayho" (1975), "Sun of Mercy" (1985) and the comedy "Thank you, provoker" (1989) were staged in the regional theater. Awarded with the Order of "Honor of the Country" (2003).

Chapter I

The uniqueness of character creation in Habib Sadulla's lyrics.

Lyric poetry is the oldest form of Uzbek literature, developed at a priority level compared to other literary forms. Lyrical poetry is the type that first echoes any events in the life of society. It is known that Uzbek lyrics have a very long history. Its roots are very strong, that's why the tree of poetry, which receives nourishment from it, always grows and gives abundant fruits. Uzbek lyric is growing in the bosom of the great literature of the East. A pollination event occurs before the harvest of various fruit trees growing in a huge garden. Due to this natural phenomenon, fruits can be of different colors and shapes. This can also be attributed to poetry. According to the demand of the time, poetry also begins to produce colorful forms from time to time. As the fruits are different due to pollination, but the taste does not change, the changes in the form of poetry should not affect its content.

Habib Sadulla spent more than forty years of his life in productive work. He is one of the creators known for his poems and epics, dramatic and prose works. His works are mainly written in a modern spirit. In them, the spiritual world, thoughts, and aspirations of our people are expressed through unique poetic images and journalistic enthusiasm. Habib Sadulla is considered to be a writer who managed to bring the beauty and freshness, sincerity, spirit and peculiarities of the country where he was born and raised to our literature.

It should be noted that in the 1960s, when Habib Sadulla and other artists of his age took up a pen with great hopes and began to put their heartaches on paper, some changes were taking place in the literary process. It is impossible to ignore the fact that many artists had to write very carefully during these years. But it is also important that almost all of these creators were united in glorifying the love for the hardworking people, the Motherland, the Mother Earth, singing love, human qualities, and scenes of nature. Under the influence of such feelings, in addition to the commonality of the subject, their unique poetic gaze and poetic skills, juicy, colorful language, bright images are clearly visible. This principle can be observed in the works of Habib Sadulla.

Today, at the beginning of the 21st century, if we look at the path of our literature, we can clearly see that the 60s of the 20th century was a turning point in literature. During these years, various changes took place in the world of poetry, the principles of writing about the human personality, emotional experiences, the pain of love, emigration, the worries of life, and the complications of life without fear began to take place. The impact of this creative phenomenon quickly paid off: significant works were created in all genres of literature. Especially in poetry, a serious change and progress was evident. Literary

criticism also expressed sincere comments about the fruits of innovation in the field of poetry. In particular, the well-known literary critic Ozod Sharafiddinov wrote "Zamon,Qalb,Poeziya" (1962), he deeply summarized the various researches, progress and some defects in the lyrics of Uzbek poetry. At the same time, it is important for us that the name of Habib Sadulla was mentioned among the young talents who bring a new tone, new theme and colors to poetry, and warm thoughts were expressed about his work. At that time, the young poet was in military service, and his poems were widely seen in the press.
Consequently, Habib Sa'dulla raised high hopes in demanding critics and kind coach Mirtemir with his first exercises.
Soon after that, in the 6th issue of 1962, "Eastern Star" magazine gave samples of poems of young poets. Habib Sa'dulla's poems were also included in this poetic bouquet, which was a recognition that a new, unique talent is entering our literature.
The poet's first poetry collection was published in 1969. This book, published in the publishing house of Literature and Art named after Gafur Ghulam, was called "Breeze from the Ocean". A poem entitled "Laughter" was also included. The poet writes:

“ Who?” say, “smile”, who doesn't love
Dear people?What's enough for a laugh,
I want to see a smile on every face
Laughter is also healing…

In these verses, "Habib Sa'dulla's later poems contain the elegance, grace, sincerity and goodness, strong pathos and the gloss of lyrical style."
Later, his book "Conversation with Spring" (1975) was published.

Lyricism is often dominated by withdrawal, emotion, or rather, a new idea hidden behind emotions. Sincere and passionate poems about the era, homeland, contemporaries, define the poet's ideological and artistic world, and also define his life position.
The creative process is very mysterious and complicated. That is why creativity in the literal sense is always individual and unique. However, no matter how individual and unique the creative process may be, there is a common law of interdependence between form and content, and there is also a general criterion of innovation, in our opinion.
The innovative nature of creativity is determined by the artistic exploration of new scenes of life and reality, new aspects, new layers of the human heart and spiritual world. In particular, the novelty of the content, the aesthetic ideal and the novelty of the idea created in this process determine the innovative nature of artistic creation.
The researches of different poetic genres and forms will acquire a meaningful essence only if they are researched in syncretic harmony with the new aspects of life and reality, with the development of the era and society, with the destiny of man and mankind, and if this poetic research is illuminated in new ideological-aesthetic and philosophical generalizations.
Usually, poetic simplicity is different. There is a high art of simplicity in Habib Sa'dulla's lyrics, which is the result of an inspiring search and creative work. Simplicity is the fruit of the organic unity of poetic form and content. In order to achieve this perfection and completeness, the great creative efforts of the poet are not felt so much, it is as if the poem was written just then, as if it flowed from the heart, as if it poured from the depths of the soul. However, this poetic simplicity is a product of the mature skill of the poet.
Habib Sa'dulla's poems "Water and Life", "Conversation with Spring" can be said to be pillars of the early poetry of life, homeland, soldier's life, love, longing, emigration, new year, art singer.

They say, "Don't spend your life like water." After all, water is the blood in the vein of life. "Life in the garden" is also from him. The poet says:

May my life be as lively as water
I agree there are a thousand!

In the poem "Conversation with Spring", the poet complains to spring, "You made me tired", and spring says, "Don't think it's easy for me", "I have worked so hard until I come out of winter". This poem enriches our thoughts. It is no exaggeration to say that the poems "My mother tongue", "Your flame", "A letter to my friend" are very rich.

In the poet's poems, natural scenery is an object that complements the image of the Motherland, not just a detail. For the poet, nature is a part of the Motherland, the basis of emotional experiences and human strength, and finally, a symbol of life that is constantly renewed and shining. Habib Sa'dulla's lyrical hero is immersed in the beauty of nature and does not disappear in the bosom of its joyful song, nature is embodied as a fair truth in the feeling of the rhythms of today's life flow and the aesthetic assessment of the process of events. Even in the poet's childhood memories, natural features directly participate in creating the spirit and passions of the time with their bright colors and lines. In particular, the nature scenes do not simply reflect the soul scenes of the lyrical hero, but under the influence of life and reality, they gain harmony with the series of experiences, emotions, and thoughts of the lyrical hero. For this reason, it seems to the poet that the khazans - "saffron leaves" that are falling to the ground one by one yesterday, are "joining the soil" and that the sycamore has no power to hold them:

The saffron leaves are plucked one by one,
He fell to the ground in a sad mood.
They were a sight yesterday,alone
What about today?

In this respect, the next verses of the poem are also characteristic and invite the reader to philosophical observation:

Not even a single leaf to hold
The strength of the great maple was not enough,
Zabardast stretched out his hands everywhere,
yellow autumn unconscious from work.

It is difficult to call Habib Sadulla a singer of nature or a poet-artist of nature. There are not many pure landscape poems in his lyrics. However, the poet and nature appear in a dialectical relationship in terms of the fact that nature feels the immortality of life and, on this basis, becomes the spiritual-philosophical criterion of things and beings, human life, aliveness.
At first glance, these ideas seem to be compatible, and an objection may be raised that "can the landscape be absent in the poet's lyrics if there are words about autumn, spring, night, and nature." The fact is that in the poet's poems, nature does not appear as an object of a special image. Although in the poems of the poet nature is present in the form of vivid details, it serves to express the psychological picture and the content of situations. This case does not occupy a leading position in the interpretation of man and nature in the poet's lyrics. In the lyrics of Habib Sa'dulla, the embodiment of human aspects in the signs of nature is shown in the first place.
Nature not only determines the physical basis of human existence and life, but also the main support of spiritual life. In the lyrics of Habib Sa'dulla, the inseparable points of man and nature have such a philosophical place.
Poems such as "Uzbekistan is a paradise" and "Uzbekistan" embody before our eyes the poetic history of the past of the Motherland, the important signs of the stages of development, and create a landscape of the experiences and feelings of our contemporaries in relation to the era and reality. The poet interprets the points of our contemporaries related to the past, the nation, the future, the fate of the mother planet in a beautiful

poetic way, and in this way reveals the spiritual responsibility to man and humanity, the mother earth and the whole earth, and the foundations of spiritual and psychological connection.

Habib Sa'dulla's lyrics give priority to lively reflection on social and spiritual issues in life. One of the characteristic features of Habib Sadulla's style is the creation of poetic images based on the facts of life. He creates deep thoughts from the facts, high-spirited ideas from the essence of the situation. Melodies from the world flow into the heart of the lyrical hero of the poet, while he evaluates the aesthetic properties of today's reality, he approaches it from the perspective of history.

An endless list of heroes,
He is full of pride.
Those brave men are the king of brave men
He is a world hero Amir Temur,
This is a rare feat in courage,
Uzbekistan is a paradise.

Habib Sadulla is constantly sought in the path of poetic exploration of new layers of life realities and hearts of our contemporaries. For this, he finds new means of expression in order to ensure that the poem reaches a wide audience, that is, he pays special attention to enriching the lines of the poem with intellectual and emotional images. That's why his lyrics, mixed with deep experiences and dark thoughts, evoke deep feelings and thoughts in the reader.

It is known that literature is the art of words. It is the great responsibility of every poet to select the most beautiful words in our language and bring them to literature and create miracles. The creator should appreciate the word like a diamond and discover its new facets. In particular, through the poetry of Habib Sa'dulla, we can witness that the word "head" has several nuances of meaning.

In the Uzbek language, the word "head" means the part of the body above the neck, the head. It can be seen that this word is appropriately used to express other meanings in the poet's poetry.

In our language, the expression "to raise one's head" is used in the meaning of "to sprout, to sprout". The poet creates a beautiful scene by bringing it to life in the following verses:

A tulip on a mountain with a raised head,
He woke up,
Misli opened his eyes out of ignorance
Speak your mind and your pride.

In the verses, the blooming of tulips and the awakening of the hills symbolically indicate the awakening of mankind from ignorance. The poet expresses the meaning of respect as follows:

I came to you again, bow your head,
Filled with zeal to justify your service.
Innocent and gentle like a seven-year-old child,
And seventeen years old fell in love.

The phrase "bow down" means that the lyrical hero bows his head due to his sense of indebtedness to humanity, the people, that is, he shows respect to his people. In this place, the lyrical hero, ready to serve and bowing his head, is compared to a seven-year-old "innocent and meek" child and a seventeen-year-old "fire lover". In turn, the seven-year-old "innocent and gentle" boy and the seventeen-year-old "fire lover" created a unique art of confrontation.

The phrase "bow down" used in the following verses does not convey the feeling of indebtedness as above, but rather conveys a sense of deep respect:

Your hands are always on your chest,
Bend your head, bend your waist,
You are so humble
High human honor.

Although the same expression is used, the bowing of the head in the verse is not only respectful but also suggestive. This situation is just one example of the subtlety of meaning in our language:

When love is in someone's heart,
When selling someone's head.

In the above verses, the meaning of "to put a bargain on the head" is meant, that is, because of love, the lover suffers a lot of pain and suffering:

What's wrong with this?
What a pain it is,
O mind, heed,
When you don't come.

In this place, the poet, through his characteristic metaphorical movement, emphasized the old age of nature and witnessed difficulties and trials for many periods, and pointed to some situations of the time:

Heads up are to blame
From your ancestors.
Your history is glorious,
Appreciate the glory.

It is necessary to appreciate the honor achieved as a result of the struggle and rebellion of our ancestors over many years in the history. Here, the expression "to raise one's head" means "to fight against".

Our people use the expression "I carry on my head" in relation to the people they respect and love and their relatives. And in these verses it is presented in a more amplified form:

Honor of covenant,
Dear beloved,
Put a crown on my head, Habib,
On the day of the arrival of delicate ado.

It is the dream of a lover not only to carry a dildo on his head, but also to wear a crown on his head and show unlimited respect.

"Bakht kushi" is a figurative image, meaning "bringer of good fortune". Its landing on the head means to be happy. The verses express the lover's desire to make his beloved happy every moment in exchange for his loyalty, love and sweet wasli.

My mother writes: "Are you healthy, my child?"
"Are you safe?" he asked...

"How are you?" is used among our people to mean "how are you?" In this place, too, the husband asks about the health of his body and soul, and asks about his condition through the word "head". The use of "head" is a sign of a man's infinite respect for his lover.

In our language, we use the phrase "to be very happy" and "to be very excited":

My head is blue
If the hand burns with passion,
Ayo is seventeen years old
The flower is long, if you are next to me.

It is a great happiness for a lover to be next to a flower-faced girl at the age of puberty, as well as "when the hand burns with passion", his joy reaches the sky. In this poem by Habib Sa'dulla, about a lover:

You are my spring of happiness,
I can't throw dice on your head.
I'm sorry, my love
Too much, don't be lazy,
If you have collected all your life
It's worth the trouble to smoke,
You have an invisible shield
When your head hits the pillow.

Even if you have worked hard all your life and accumulated wealth, when your head is on the pillow, your wealth is not visible to your eyes, it does not fit your heart, says the poet. Even this phrase is included in the title of the poem. The poet reinforces the conclusion of long-term life observations by repeating at the end of each stanza.

Habib Sadulla's poetry is meaningful and prolific. In order to find the face of a word, to discover new facets of the so-called diamond, a poet, in the words of Abdulla Qahhor, needs "something else" besides talent and hard work. Along with talent and hard work, Habib Sa'dulla has "something else" that makes every word shine like a diamond in the poet's poems.

Chapter II
Image of nature and its role in revealing human character

The word is a miracle. The word is a means of understanding the state, mentality, and heart of another. The word is a magical weapon that infects human senses. The word is the interpreter of the inner and outer world of a person. But he can achieve these qualities only by riding the horse of thought. Therefore, the word is life-giving in its deep meaning, just as the female race is beautiful with its beautiful dress, river bank, and nature is beautiful and lush with its trees. The power, beauty, meaning, and impact of words are clearly visible, especially in poetry. . Russian poet L. Nekrasov wrote the following words in the margin of the manuscript of one of his poems: "A simile is poetry, a picture is poetry, an event can be poetic, nature is poetry, emotion is poetry." Nature, like all art forms and genres, is one of the eternal themes of lyrics. No matter which of the works of art we choose, in the image of the landscape in it, of course, a person participates, one or another property of nature is rediscovered through the human relationship to it; for this reason, the nature pictures in the artistic work are full of emotional color.

In this sense, the landscape serves as a background and at the same time an organic cell for the bright embodiment of human feelings and experiences in the lyrics.

Nowadays, the artistic research of the complex inner world of the human character, the manifestations of the spiritual world in connection with the events of life, with a high intellectual capacity and philosophical depth, is gaining special importance. Of course, it is impossible to study the researches of a number of poets like Habib Sa'dulla separately from the experience of teachers and the traditions of classical poetry.

The alternation of the seasons of nature is a requirement of the immutable law of dialectics inherent in the eternal nature. Likewise, each season paves the way for another season to emerge. You want to apply this situation directly to the literary process. Even in literature, including our poetry, a wave of new generations is taking place over time. As the representatives of each generation create their own artistic world with their own voice, style, manner, ideological-aesthetic principles, theme, this feature determines the appearance and nature of this generation. Characterization of their place and role in the development of the poetry of this period, their contribution to the development of artistic and aesthetic thinking makes it possible to think about the general development of our poetry at this stage. In particular, the poetics and creative researches of each new generation are characterized by unique historical conditions and new social reality. The mutual differentiation and dissimilarity of these social realities is manifested in the construction of images in the artistic work, in the aesthetic function of poetic images, and in the differentiation of poets' works.

Nowadays, the artistic research of the complex inner world of the human character, the manifestations of the spiritual world in connection with the events of life, with a high intellectual capacity and philosophical depth, is gaining special importance. Of course, it is impossible to study the researches of a number of poets like Habib Sa'dulla separately from the experience of teachers and the traditions of classical poetry. Relying on the experiences of the genius artists of the past, creating wonderful poetic works that incorporate the reality of the 20th century and the innovations of social life into their essence, and in the process, connecting the best features of the past tradition with the innovation created by themselves, has risen to a new level in our current poetry. In particular, this direction is particularly noticeable in the works of Habib Sadulla.

It plays a leading role in the enrichment of the creative world of poets, the expansion of the worldview of each artist, the formation of aesthetic principles, and the widening of the scope of thinking.

When a poet is writing about a subject, he is certainly motivated by events, nature, feelings, thoughts and experiences. The poem should have a form that always fascinates the heart of the reader, gives him aesthetic pleasure, and brings him into the personal world of sophistication. How successfully a poem is written depends in many ways on the experiences of the poet.

A poem lives only when it is written from the heart, with pure inspiration. We even come across opinions that a real poem is written with a stroke. It is related to the state of mind and is called lyrical experience in literary studies. Lyrical experience is called instant lyrical experience and memory lyrical experience depending on the presence of emotional, intellectual and simple thinking.

People's writer of Uzbekistan, Hero of Uzbekistan Said Ahmed's drawings about Habib Sadulla reflect on the history of creation of ghazal.

Habib Sadulla, writing about himself, noted that he had the opportunity to talk with famous authors of our literature, as well as Saeed Ahmed, and learn from them.

The alternation of the seasons of nature is a requirement of the immutable law of dialectics inherent in the eternal nature. Likewise, each season paves the way for another season to emerge. You want to apply this situation directly to the literary process. Even in literature, including our poetry, a wave of new generations is taking place over time. As the representatives of each generation create their own artistic world with their own voice, style, manner, ideological-aesthetic principles, theme, this feature determines the appearance and nature of this generation. Characterization of their place and role in the development of the poetry of this period, their contribution to the development of artistic and aesthetic thinking makes it possible to think about the general development of our poetry at this stage. In particular, the poetics and creative researches of each new generation are characterized by unique historical conditions and new social reality. The mutual differentiation and dissimilarity of these social realities is manifested in the construction of images in the artistic work, in the aesthetic function of poetic images, and in the differentiation of poets' works.

Nowadays, the artistic research of the complex inner world of the human character, the manifestations of the spiritual world in connection with the events of life, with a high intellectual capacity and philosophical depth, is gaining special importance. Of course, it is impossible to study the researches of a number of poets like Habib Sadulla separately from the experience of teachers and the traditions of classical poetry. Relying on the experiences of the genius artists of the past, creating wonderful poetic works that incorporate the reality of the 20th century and the innovations of social life into their essence, and in the process, connecting the best features of the past tradition with the innovation created by themselves, has risen to a new level in our current poetry. In particular, this direction is particularly noticeable in the works of Habib Sadulla.

It plays a leading role in the enrichment of the creative world of poets, the expansion of the worldview of each artist, the formation of aesthetic principles, and the widening of the scope of thinking.

When a poet is writing about a subject, he is certainly motivated by events, nature, feelings, thoughts and experiences. The poem should have a form that always fascinates the heart of the reader, gives him aesthetic pleasure, and brings him into the personal world of sophistication. How successfully a poem is written depends in many ways on the experiences of the poet.

A poem lives only when it is written from the heart, with pure inspiration. We even come across opinions that a real poem is written with a stroke. It is related to the state of mind and is called lyrical experience in literary studies. Lyrical experience is called instant lyrical experience and memory lyrical experience depending on the presence of emotional, intellectual and simple thinking.

People's writer of Uzbekistan, Hero of Uzbekistan Said Ahmed's drawings about Habib Sadulla reflect on the history of creation of ghazal.

Habib Sadulla, writing about himself, noted that he had the opportunity to talk with famous authors of our literature, as well as Saeed Ahmed, and learn from them.

Literary scholar Erkin Khudoyberdiev said: "This ghazal is a vivid example of amazing grace and charm, exaggeration mixed with cheerful humor."

The ghazal begins with the following verses:

a wonderful smell
When a soul passes through my street,
there will be a standing dice on the trail
When a soul passes through my street.

That is, "musk ila anbar" spreads as a soul passes by the street in front of the lyrical hero. In the eyes of a lover, the dirt on the trail turns into dice. The poet writes his feelings to the pen. He tries to justify his thoughts with life details, so that when we read the ghazal, a reasonable situation in harmony with natural scenes is embodied before our eyes. In this passage, which uses the art of diagnosis, which is created by animating and personifying things and events in nature, the lyric expresses the mental state of the hero when he crosses the street:

To be an umbrella over his head
A wall overhanging in hope,
The branches bow down
When a soul passes through my street.

Planting trees next to the wall is a real life phenomenon, as the wall leans over the street and casts a shadow - the poet enlivens the landscape under the influence of a momentary lyrical experience as follows: "As the soul passes through the street with love, the trees and branches bow down to it like people over the wall in the dream of being an umbrella." In addition, there is a proverb in our people: "If your neighbor sows fruit, knock down the wall" - because it is a local color, we accept verses quickly and easily.
The following verses are a sign of the boundless emotions of the lyrical hero:

Give life to the wall
But the stones are melting.
If you look once,
When a soul passes through my street.

That is, if the soul turns its gaze once, the soul enters the wall. The poet exaggerates that even the stones piled on its foundation will melt. As the saying goes, "stones will melt" and where there is love, evil will disappear. But in its own sense, if we analyze life, it is clear that if the stone melts, the wall will fall. The wall, of course, falls towards the street. In the eyes of the poet, it seems as if he is resting on the shore, and he is given life. This is a great example of animation art.

As the poet continues the series of events, he connects their sequence to each other by using the art of tashbehi silsilaiband, an example of a chain. A lover dreams of becoming a wall so that he can calmly see the beauty of his lover:

look at his face
If I die when I leave the wall,
Laughter is crazy about me
When a soul passes through my street

It should also be noted that the expression "to become a wall" also means "to become numb", "to lose oneself". After seeing the beauty of his lover, the lover, numb as a wall, falls at the foot of the river, and even laughs at the willows. The state of a lover is worse than that of a madman. The mental state of the poet after immediate lyrical experiences is revealed very clearly and clearly by using the art of metaphor in these verses.

In order to analyze the following verses, we will again refer to the memoirs of Said Ahmed.

"On that day, Habib Sa'dulla was staring at a leech crossing the street, and the passengers on the street said:

- Look at the man who saw two sword-like boys staring at a woman! That's why the people of Namangan don't let their daughters go out alone!"

Even if it rains on his head, it's a mess,
My job is to travel, however
It's better not to look
When a soul passes through my street.

The creator's experience can form simple thoughts. But he chooses what is suitable for his work, separates the most important and poetic aspects. The selected edge becomes an artistic entity that carries the stream of lyrical experience and expresses its vibrations in one direction or another. Above we witnessed the artistic expression of these ideas. Since the reality in the poem is the poet's own experiences, the lyrical hero is the poet himself. Now the lyrical hero looks forward to tomorrow with hope:

You put your life on the road,
Habib, stop, don't despair,
Days come after night,
When a soul passes through my street.

At the end of the above stanzas, the radif "When a soul passes by my street" is a poetic expression of a situation, pouring out emotions, revealing the essence of this event, or creating a speech structure around certain traditional concepts, images, images, expressions, grace is the fruit of the intention to show.
In fact, there's no other way than to turn it into a fire-breathing lion to save instant lyrical experiences. Most of the great works of Uzbek poetry are works created directly in the wake of immediate lyrical experience. That's why Habib Sadulla's ghazal "When a life passes from my street" fills the hearts of fans with beautiful feelings. As the beautiful expression of the image of nature used in the ghazal sinks into the heart of the poet's passionate and sincere confession, the reader seeks to understand the secret of the poet's personality, thinking and the feelings of the lyrical hero, which is the result of the strange magic of poetry.

Art has been discovering new features of nature at every socio-historical stage of human development. In the process of perceiving the properties of nature, our poets take food from it to illuminate their ideals. In this respect, the images of modernity, nature, motherland, and the holy land are embodied in poetic works as a reflection of social goals and specific ideas.

Let's look at Habib Sadulla's poem "In the Garden".

My heart is slow
A scarf over her face,
A scarf from the face,
Her face looked inside the garden.

Dilbar walks slowly into the garden and takes his scarf from his face. Her face and grace are so beautiful that even a flower is amazed. Here is a great example of diagnostic art:

"Wow, it's amazing, it's a blessing."
Will that be enough?!"
He opened his mouth and said,
Gulshan became a flower lol.

In this place, the landscape is subordinated to a specific ideological-aesthetic goal in harmony with the feelings and thoughts of the lyrical hero. Landscape image of the outside world.

Through the image of nature, the images of our motherland, we get to know the deep feelings and thoughts of the poet, as well as his deep thoughts about the era, reality, people, life, and the place of the new man in reality. In such works, nature becomes not only a background, but an integral part of the general idea and content of the work, and to a certain extent it becomes a part of the poet's experiences, the idea and content that he wants to promote.

We accept every landscape poem of Habib Sadulla as his lyrical confession. In the poet's poems, the landscape is described as absorbing the human spirit, love, pain, joy, essence, and emotional experiences. All poetic devices serve this purpose. In the image of Habib Sa'dulla, night, evening, spring waters, dew, swallows, meadows and other factors affect the reader, evoke emotional experience and thoughts, and through them the poet reveals the human heart, the inner world of a person:

Brides are seen in apricot blossoms,
Ibo, elegance in innocent buds,
A smile that shines on the face of the sun,
Unparalleled freshness in the layer of rays,
Nowruz is
It's the festive season.

It seems that the role of the landscape in the lyrics is very wide and varied. It cultivates our aesthetic taste by revealing the beauty in the nature of things and objects around us; it is also embodied as a symbol of our motherland, its poetic images.

Poetic study of the subject of nature and man, as noted above, is inextricably linked with the development of the socio-political and intellectual thinking of our people. In this regard, literary critic H. Yakubov's "images of nature and social life enrich our imagination of humanities and our knowledge of the nature of man to a certain extent by how the poet looks at them (how he understands them). His opinion that the poet creates a lyrical form of character by expressing his attitude to the phenomenon of reality (whether it is a natural or a social phenomenon) is very reasonable.

If there is even a tiny example of a person in the boundless nature; in the face of the cruel steps of time, when he thinks of the momentary life, he feels so much in the face of death; otherwise, what is the meaning of life if it is given only once; How does a person feel connected to nature? From the poetic answer given to these questions, we learn about the character of our contemporaries, the richness of their spiritual and psychological world, and the social importance of the activities of our contemporaries. Today, the topic of nature and man is

one of the most important issues due to its socio-economic and spiritual nature.
The responsibility of protecting the environment, nature, creating a great future of the country using the energy and enthusiasm of youth, and transferring its benefits to future generations became an expression of love for the motherland, people, people, and the Motherland. appears as:

This season brings love, dreams, song,
Able to restore youth.
Holding a flower in her arms,
It also wakes up tomorrow,
The spring of my country is
Flowering season is.

The poet's lyrical hero is a true patriot. Spring awakens enthusiasm and enthusiasm in his heart, confidence in the future. He is proud that the spring of his country is full of flowers.
Nature, a living being, consists of certain contradictions arising from its law; it is not easy to catch the moment of their harmonious harmony. Habib Sa'dulla knows and understands the essence of these delicate moments, in his poems he interprets the depth and beauty hidden in the essence of these delicate moments in harmony with life, man, life and eternity. In this process, the mood and tone of the lyricism, the immortality of life, the goodness of human life, in short, the philosophical interpretation of the essence of life and being alive become clear. The poet is not speaking on behalf of an entire generation on earth with pompous and sonorous words. He is thinking about his soul experiences, feelings, thoughts, worries, joys. But, the most important thing is that you can feel the breath of the era, the heartbeat of the era. He can express the hardworking image of Uzbek people in simple words:

That's it,
Don't call a hero.
A small step into space.

"Father" in the cotton field
An ordinary Uzbek man.
please write a poem
Do not interpret the number as a reporter.
Don't be glittery
Indeed
Show me the hardworking man.

The formal aspect of the poem deserves special attention. Because this formal style, along with giving a unique tone, enhances emotionality and shows subtleties of meaning.
Lyric is like a floor. In particular, in the bosom of the mother earth, which gave strength to sprouted grasses, herbs, flowers, and sedariahons, the great maples also took firm root; besides the tall height of the flowers, there is also a loud rustle and sound of the maple trees. This, in itself, shows the extent and power of the earth. In this sense, the scope of interest and expression of today's Uzbek lyrics has expanded tremendously, in its bosom, poems written about the socio-political reality of our time are the main ones, along with the expression of feelings that reveal the human character, such as peace, intimate-love melodies, the description of nature and landscape, gentle moods and situations. takes place; it is these who have a leading position in defining the image of today's Uzbek lyrics; it is these that represent the character of the epic that is manifested in the nature of our lyrics. In the following poem by Habib Sa'dulla, the lyrical hero supposedly talks to the spring:

- You hit your chest saying I missed you,
Don't think it's easy for me either.
I suffered a lot, I suffered a lot,
Until he comes out of the depths of hell...

In this place, there is a connection between nature and man, and spring is a metaphorical lover. Lover's agony is revealed through natural phenomena. This harmony comes to the poet and shapes his feeling.

In poetic works, the poetic thought is always in an emotional color, and feelings are illuminated by the light of thought. This kind of harmony of emotion and opinion is one of the main laws of lyrics; it originates from the original nature of lyric poetry and constitutes its essence. V. G. Belinsky, showing the characteristic features of lyric poetry, writes: "This is the kingdom of subjectivity, this inner world is the world of initiatives that stay inside and do not go out. In this, poetry remains within the realm of feeling and consciousness in the inner element; in this, the soul hides behind the external reality, and presents to poetry the incomparable glimmers of the inner life that reflects the external world. In this, the personality of the poet is in the first place, we accept and understand everything only through him.

Habib Sa'dulla's skills, originality and evocative power of his poems are such that they do not drag the reader into depressing experiences and a vortex of ineffective thoughts. While poetically researching the eternity of life and the goodness of human life, he puts forward the philosophy of giving beauty and eternity to the short life that everyone has been given, and on this basis, values the passing life and ensures its eternity, and sings a song of joy:

Then my sorrow fell into the sea
The drop is absorbed like an oil.
As if the sun rises in the evening,
Joy overcomes sadness.

Above, a strange example of the landscape invites a person to philosophical reflection. In philosophical lyrics, the image of nature does not become a separate image object, separated from the human, social life, spiritual and psychological world of the person.

Philosophical lyrics also explore nature and man in a harmonious relationship. The reason is that although man appears as a power that subjugates nature to his will, he is actually a child of nature, a conscious member of nature.

Although the aesthetic, emotional and moral aspects of the relationship between man and nature are of some interest to the poet in the philosophical lyrics, this is not the priority in the philosophical poem; In this place, for the poet, the idea arising from the connection between nature and man is important. Here, too, the poet focuses on the essence created by the requirement of the harmonious relationship between nature and man:

Being gathered the blanket of winter,
Spring under the snow has awakened.
Languages repeat the philosophy of love,
Lovers wake up in love,
This is a pain reliever.
Tis the season.

In the lyrics of Habib Sadulla, the creative ideas of our contemporaries, high ideals of living and working, beliefs and professions resonate in harmony. That's why Habib Sa'dulla's lyrics can be said to be a philosophical interpretation, an artistic vision of the spiritual and intellectual life of our contemporaries. Every poem of Habib Sadulla is literally always filled with actual and deep social content. The poet's poetry fulfills ideological and aesthetic tasks such as revealing the character of a person, encouraging life through pure work and good faith, and encouraging one to confidently step into the future.

CONCLUSION

People's poet of Uzbekistan Habib Sa'dulla was a great wordsmith who contributed to the development of Uzbek literature for many years. He was always at the service of the nation, and observed the events happening in the social life of our people with vigilance and intelligence. The hero of the lyric expressed his experiences through various emotions. Listening to the hearts of his contemporaries, he tried to sing with sensitivity their dreams, optimistic goals, moral and educational views.

Many poems and ghazals created by Habib Sadulla have become the property of poetry lovers today. Many poems have taken a firm place in the repertoires of hafiz and are becoming songs in every household. These poems and songs have given peace to the hearts of thousands of people and propagate the ideas of goodness, nobility, honesty, purity, hard work, justice and truth.

The prolific lyrics of the poet, the poems "Tazarru" and "Jarohat", the drama "Yusuf and Zulayho" are a worthy contribution to the development of Uzbek literature. The "Ramadan Prayer", "Spring Inspirations" series, "Shukrona", a collection of poems and epics published at the end of his life, clearly demonstrated that Habib Sadulla was one of the best artists of words, and that ten inspirations were added to one inspiration in the conditions of the new era, freedom. The publication of the two-volume "Selected Works" opened a wide way to research and analysis of his work, created great opportunities for scientific research.

When we read examples of Habib Sa'dulla's work, we feel that every line of his works breathes life, and reality is described objectively and truthfully. It's not for nothing, of course. Along with his artistic work, the poet has been serving the nation for many years. No matter where he worked, no matter what front he led, he never left the virtues of diligence, diligence, and honesty. This was especially evident during the years when he worked as a deputy of the Oliy Majlis.

It is natural that every artist stops working on himself, gets tired of research, gets stuck somewhere, cannot rise from the ladders of the high peaks of creativity. When we look at the creative heritage of Habib Sadulla, we can see that he created prolifically in every season of his life, and was in sync with the era and time. The enthusiasm, sincerity, and inspiration during the years of research and experience acquisition during the years when he entered the field of literature continued continuously in the later stages of his life. Also, over the years, the poet's pen sharpened ideologically and philosophically, and his social views, attitude to life and living became more and more serious, deep and impressive. This is one of the unique qualities that not all pen people have.

t is known that many facets of the author's personality are objectively reflected in the lyrical hero. While we are talking about the poet's personal qualities and characteristics, we must admit that we have unintentionally relied on the poet's biographical information in elucidating the character of the lyrical hero, which is the subject of our research. Characteristics of the poet's lyrical hero: generosity, patriotism, fortitude, generosity, etc., it can be felt that, first of all, there are traits of the poet's personality and character.

Since Habib Sa'dulla began his work by writing poems, his skill in lyrical genre, genres, methods of expression, and image tools grew from work to work, from book to book. Over the years, the range of topics and ideas of his work expanded more and more. The range of lyrical images is enriched accordingly. Continuity of gradual improvement in the depiction of spiritual experiences, deepening of ideological-philosophical conclusions in his creative activity was of great importance. The system of genres also expanded and improved. The poet, who tried his pen in more quatrains and traditional ghazals, gradually tried his strength in simple and combined weights. Aruz used his opportunities to cover modern topics. Poetry translation served him as an additional experience and school of learning. He tried to say something new about the themes and motives of the homeland, work, science, youth, love, migration.

The poet, who perfectly mastered various tools and methods to reveal the character traits of the lyrical hero in poetry, was able to demonstrate his skills in epic poetry. The poems "Birth Year", "Living Victims", "Onaizor" introduced Habib Sadulla's name to literature lovers thanks to his prolific creativity in lyrical genres. The dramas "Yusuf and Zulayho" and "Sun of Mercy" became important events in our cultural life as a perfect literary heritage as a result of the combination of epic image and deep lyricism.

At the end of our research work, we came to the following general conclusions:

1. Habib Sa'dulla is the author of the pen who was able to make a worthy contribution to the development of Uzbek literature not only with his lyrical but also with his epic works.
2. The poet did not deviate from the principles of modernity when creating the character of the lyrical hero. Based on the specifics and characteristics of the lyrical genre to which he is referring, he effectively and appropriately used various methods and means of character creation.
3. Habib Sadulla is a writer who is well aware of the history and present of the art of speech. That is why, while successfully continuing the traditions started by the poets of the past, he gave them a modern spirit, raised and developed the traditions to a new level.
4. Habib Sadulla's literary heritage fully meets the requirements of the era and time in terms of genres, themes and ideas, as well as artistic and moral-educational features. Consequently, he can easily provide material for future scientific researches on the artistic works of his pen.

References:

1. Karimov I. A. High spirituality is an irresistible force. -T: "Uzbekistan" publishing house. -2008.
2. Karimov I. A. The idea of national independence: basic concepts and principles. -T: "Uzbekistan" publishing house. 2000
3. Literary types and genres. Roof II. Roof 1. UzR FA. -T: "Fan" publishing house. 1991
4. Literary types and genres. Roof II. 2nd floor. UzR FA. -T: "Fan" publishing house. 1992
5. Aristotle. Poetics -T: G'. Ghulam Literature and Art Publishing House. 1980
6. Asalliev A., Rahmonov F. The charm of fine art. -T: Literary and art publishing house named after Gafur Ghulam. 1974
7. Belinsky V.G. Selected works. -T: "Uzdavnashr" publishing house. 1955
8. Boboev T. Basics of literary studies. -T: "Uzbekistan" publishing house. 2002
9. Boborahimov. M. Conflict and character and Uzbek lyric 80th anniversary. Author's dissertation. 1991
10. "Book of Youth". Poetry, prose, translation, literary studies.-T: ShNMAK. 2008
11. Team. Literary theory. Roof II. Volume 1.-T: "Fan" publishing house. 1978
12. Dzhorakulov U. Boundless jingle. -T: "Fan" publishing house. 2006
13. Joraev H. Lyrical character and personality of the author. -T: "Fan" publishing house. 2008
14. Komilov N. A conflict of life and death. Ghazals. Comments. -T: 1991
15. Mallaev N. History of Uzbek literature. -T: "Teacher" publishing house. 1976
16. Mamajonov S. The world of the poet. -T: Literary and art publishing house named after Gafur Ghulam. 1974
17. Nazarov B. Vitality is a beautiful criterion.-T: "Yosh gvardiya" publishing house. 1985

18. Olimjon H. Selected works. Three roofs. 3rd floor. Pages 132-141.
19. Panasenko E.D., Umarov E.A. Spelling dictionary of the Uzbek language. -T: Publishing House of the World of Economics and Law. 1998
20. Rahimjonov N. Period and Uzbek lyrics. -T: "Fan" publishing house. 1979
21. Sultan I. Literary theory.-T: "Teacher" publishing house. 1980.
22. Solijonov Y. Scrutinizing eyes of truth. -T: Publishing House of the National Library of Uzbekistan named after Alisher Navoi. 2009 Pages 158-167.
23. Solijonov Y. Current Uzbek lyrics. "Fergana" publishing house. 2009
24. Sarimsakov B. N. Basics and criteria of literary studies. -T: A. Akhmedova printing house. 2004
25. Sadullaev H. Selected works. I roof. -T: Chief editorial office of "Sharq" publishing joint-stock company. 2002
26. Sadullaev H. Selected works. Volume II. -T: Chief editorial office of "Sharq" publishing joint-stock company. 2002
27. Soliev A. The psyche of the hero and the dramatic situation. UzAS. 2008. Issue 4.
28. Turdieva K. Nature and spirituality. UzAS. 1990.
29. Toychiev U. Literary types and genres. Roof III. Volume II.-T: "Fan" publishing house. 1992
30. Khrapchenko M.B. Tvorcheskaya individualnost pisatelya i razvitie literatury.-M: 1970 g.
31. An anthology of 20th century Uzbek poetry. National encyclopedia of Uzbekistan State Scientific Publishing House. 2007
32. Khudoyberdiev E. Habib Sadulla. -T: "World of Creativity" publishing house. 2004
33. Sharofiddinov O. Talent shines. -T: Literature and art. 1976
34. Sheikhzadeh M. Works. Roof VI. Volume IV.-T: Literature and art. 1979
35. Sheikhzadeh M. About Navoi's lyrical hero. Great Uzbek poet. -T: Literature and art. 1984

36. An explanatory dictionary of the Uzbek language. National encyclopedia of Uzbekistan. Tashkent. 2006. Volume 1.
37. Koshjanov M. Creative responsibility. -T: Literature and art. 1981.
38. Kuronov D. "Literature is rare" or the shepherd's eternal question. -T: "Zarqalam" publishing house. 2006.
39. Gafurov I. Hayo is the savior. -T: "Fan" publishing house. 2006
40. Haqqul I. The love of independence and the fate of the individual.-T: UzAS. 1995. Issue 3.
41. Hamdamov U. The need for renewal. -T: "Fan" publishing house. 2006
42. Hayitmetov A. From the footsteps of Tabarruk. -T: Literary and art publishing house named after Gafur Ghulam. 1979
43. Hojiahmedov A. Poetic arts and classical rhyme. -T: "Sharq" publishing house. 1998
44. Hotamov N., Sarimsakov B. Russian-Uzbek explanatory dictionary of literary terms. -T: "Teacher" publishing house. 1979
45. Hojiahmedov A. The merit of classical artistry. -T: "Sharq" publishing house. 2002

Printed by Books on Demand GmbH, Norderstedt / Germany